PRAISE FO

"We engaged Steve to steer our strategic growth as we saw the value in making people central to decision-making. We implemented many of the ideas and strategies that Steve outlined to devastatingly good effect and it has enabled us to grow, combat the negativity of the pandemic and refocus our business. We have a firm focus on making Employee Engagement one of our key pillars going forward."

—Mark Crutchley, Chief Executive of the Circadian Trust

"We've collaborated with and endorsed Steve to numerous clients. I must say, both we and our clients have thoroughly appreciated his invaluable insights and support concerning business culture, motivation, employee engagement, and growth."

—Jessica Comolly-Jones, Director at Rubicon People Partnership

"Having worked with Steve as a consultant to measure our staff engagement and motivation, we teamed up to deliver a workshop at the Employee Ownership Association Conference in November 2023, titled 'Your Engagement and Communication Strategy'.

Whilst we intended to facilitate a discreet workshop, we ended presenting to almost a third of the conference attendees, over 250 people. It quickly became a significant talking point both at the conference, and in subsequent conversations outside of Employer Ownership.

Steve's no-nonsense approach to engagement, backed up by easy diagnosis and on-going measurement, has made a real difference to our business. Understanding our team's motivation and engagement has helped tighten our positioning, and provide the kind of work our team find most enjoyable, motivating and satisfying."

—Harry Pocknell, Strategy & Creative Director at Salad Brand+Communication

"The Enterprise M3 Growth Hub engaged with Steve to deliver business support to our clients right across the region. As well as keynote speaker appearances Steve, as part of our support activities for modern leaders, has facilitated 60 business leaders through his own Engaging Leaders Programme and the response from participants has been truly awesome! With satisfaction levels at 95%+, and a waiting list for future programmes, the outcomes have far exceeded our expectations."

—Andrew Swift, Senior Growth Champion at Enterprise M3 Growth Hub

"I had the pleasure of working with Steve and involving him to run a workshop on Employee Engagement at our event. It seemed that at times people forgot to blink, and the note-taking was intense! Steve has turned the topic of motivation from a soft concept into a tangible, achievable and measurable metric. With his own personalised frameworks, he helped our audience understand what intrinsically motivates them and their staff, where they have gone wrong and what exactly they should do the second they leave the room."

—Sibel Dbila, Content & Events Producer at Help to Grow. Small Business Charter

HOW TO BECOME AN EMPLOYER OF CHOICE

UNLEASH YOUR GROWTH THROUGH TALENT ATTRACTION AND RETENTION

STEVE JONES

FOREWORD

I am very honoured to be given the opportunity to write the foreword for this exceptional book by Steve Jones.

I first met Steve during my tenure as Director of Executive Development Programmes at Henley Business School. In a landscape saturated with business coaches and trainers, Steve stood out as refreshingly different, an authentic and insightful educator. At that time, Steve was a member of a government task group exploring the enablers of employee engagement. Steve's rigorous approach in researching his topics alongside his wealth of first-hand industry experience really does give him huge face validity and relevance when engaging with senior leaders. He is at the forefront of learning design and has designed and delivered workshops across many geographies and business sectors.

I was delighted when Steve agreed to engage with the Executive Learning Partnership audiences at Southampton Business School, University of Southampton. He was a regular contributor and a sought-after speaker, engaging with many of our clients. Steve brightens up any room with his unique perspectives, leaving an indelible impression on the audience and always leaving them with a call to action.

Fast forward to the present day, and Steve is an indispensable part of the team at the University of Winchester Business School. As a visiting executive he delivers several modules on the government backed 'Help to Grow Management' course. Here, he continues to impart his invaluable knowledge and insights, contributing significantly to the success of the course and leaving a lasting impact on the alumni.

In the pages that follow, you will discover not just a book but a culmination of Steve's experience, distilled into actionable insights and guidance. This is not a theoretical exploration; it is a practical roadmap forged through years of hands-on expertise alongside rigorous research. As you delve into the wisdom within these pages, you'll find yourself guided by a mentor who has not only been there, and done that, but is passionate about paving the way for others to follow.

Prepare to embark on a journey through the unique lens of Steve's perspectives – a journey that has been enriched by a genuine desire to empower others on their paths to success.

—Paul Bennett, Ex Director of Executive Development Programs at Henley Business School, currently Course Co-Ordinator (Help To Grow + Alumini) University of Winchester Business School.

Paul Bennett and myself at Southampton Business School.

WHY THIS BOOK AND WHY NOW?

Becoming an "Employer of Choice' has never been more important.

In the evolving landscape of leadership and organisational success, there is a real challenge for businesses and organisations to find and keep the right talent to sustain and enable growth. Never has it been more critical for leaders to navigate the complexities of managing not just employees in the limited professional sense, but the whole person.

The aftermath of the pandemic has transformed leadership roles into a holistic endeavour, entailing responsibilities for employee well-being, mental health, diversity, equality, and inclusion.

Modern leaders find themselves grappling with challenges such as "quiet quitting," the war for talent, presenteeism, the four-day workweek, and the ever-present issues of sickness and absenteeism, which carry significant financial implications. It's a complex scenario, but the good news is that it doesn't have to be this way.

In this book, I draw upon my 25 years of experience working with fast-growth businesses, including being part of the leadership team at Fitness First Plc during its remarkable journey to becoming the largest independent health club chain globally—all within a seven year period. Through the highs and lows of that fast-growth journey, I gained insights into effective leadership and the challenges it presents.

My story doesn't end there: it led me to the realisation that attracting and retaining talent is pivotal for sustained growth. This realisation prompted me to establish Skills for Business Training Ltd, focusing on motivation, leadership, and employee engagement.

The government's interest in employee engagement issues led to my involvement as co-chair of a steering committee which looked at Employee Engagement in detail and studied companies that truly were harnessing the full potential and capabilities of their people.

We identified four key themes that distinguished organisations harnessing the full potential and capabilities of their people.

The culmination of my journey, from the private sector to government collaboration, ultimately led me to write this book.

I've built it around the four enablers we found:

- Visible Empowering Leadership
- Engaging Managers and Leaders
- Employee Voice
- Organisational Integrity

These enablers form the foundation of this book. We will explore each one in detail along with the 12 key strategies derived from them.

But why now? The urgency stems from the need for leaders to not just survive but thrive in the dynamic contemporary business environment. As you embark on this journey with me, I invite you to assess your organisation's standing on these enablers using the QR code included. This quick self-assessment will guide your focus in the chapters ahead, ensuring that you gain actionable insights tailored to your specific needs.

Remember, this is just your perception and your colleagues may hold differing perceptions which will hopefully lead to healthy and productive debates and actions.

SCAN THE QR CODE:

Are you an Employer of Choice?

Find out by taking our 2-minute quiz!

"Employers of Choice attract and keep talent and are usual highly productive and profitable as an outcome."

So, let's delve into the heart of employee engagement and modern leadership, explore the four enablers, and equip ourselves with the strategies to become the employer of choice—making your organisation a place where talent not only resides but flourishes.

WHERE DID IT ALL START?

My journey into helping businesses become employers of choice by working on their employee engagement all started back in 2015, with a presentation I gave at the Vitality Stadium, Bournemouth (home of AFC Bournemouth FC).

It was to a delegation of business owners and the subject I was presenting on was Employee Engagement and Motivation.

In the audience that day was Warren Munson of Inspire Professional Services – a very forward-thinking accountancy practice.

As a result of the presentation, Warren asked me to work with his business, which at the time had around 50 employees.

Prior to starting his business, Warren had been part of one of the top four accountancy practices in London.

He'd been offered a partnership but turned it down because when he looked at many of the partners, they seemed burnt out, tired, and to some extent on the treadmill. To put it kindly, Warren wasn't inspired by what he saw.

He was, however, inspired to build his own practice where his focus was on supporting SME Business Owners to be great with his strategic accountancy practice.

All was fine in the early days as he devoted time and energy in helping business owners grow their businesses.

However, somewhere along the journey, Warren, by his own admission, took his eye off the ball and began focusing more on the money than his original intent.

Fast forward 10 years and Warren's business was beginning to look and feel like the Big Four organisation he had left.

To the outside world, he was a success. But inside, he was falling out of love with his business.

Luckily, we met and, after a year of working with Warren and his Senior Leadership team, we were able to redress the balance and build a business that Warren and his Senior Management Team were proud of once more, using many of the techniques outlined in this book. This has led to some important recognition in terms of eminent National awards. As a role model and mentor himself, Warren Munson achieved Business Leader of the Year award for the Dorset Business awards.

Regarded as one of the Dorset Business Awards' highest accolades, the Business Leader of the Year Award recognised Warren's innovative and leadership within his field.

Further, Inspire Professional Services were crowned Independent Firm of the Year for the Southwest and Wales by the British Accountancy Awards, the industry's most esteemed accolade. This prestigious title is awarded to firms with a turnover up to £3m who are able to demonstrate how they've added a significant value to their clients and across all service areas.

Inspire Professional Services followed this by scooping top place in The Accountancy Age Best Employer award, confirming them as one of the UK best places to work. Even more impressively, they were awarded 'Company Star of the Year' by Rocket Star Awards. This prestigious title is awarded to firm with fewer than 50 employees who are able to demonstrate they are hiring, training ,and nurturing young talent.

Clearly, all of this recognition was possible because Warren's vision and determination to create a workforce with a difference, an engaged workforce powered by engagement philosophy, the right mindset, and using the tools and techniques outline in this book.

It shows how far in business can evolve, a far cry from the dark days when Warren had questioned where the business was heading.

Fast forward to current day and Warren has successfully sold his business but continues to work with companies to help them grow in his new business aptly titled Evolve.

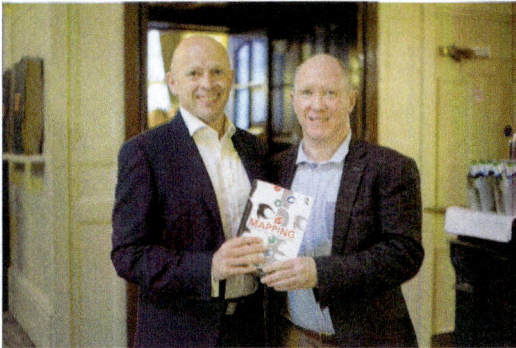

Warren Munson and myself at the launch of Mapping Motivation for Engagement.

Having enjoyed seeing the transformation of his business, Warren introduced me to one of his clients Aish Technologies.

Aish Technologies is a systems design and manufacturing company specialising in the protection of electronic equipment in harsh environments.

Based in Poole, Aish had full engineering, manufacturing, and installation capability that supported customers from concept design through to full installation.

When I started working with the Board and Senior Management Team their goal was to show commitment to supporting and developing its 240 employees and delivering success.

It wasn't easy, because Aish at the time were a second-generation business with their son, Lloyd Bates, taking the reins from his father. Therefore, we had old school and new school thinking to content with—those who wanted a new way of working and those that didn't. For our endeavour to succeed, we needed unity across the board, senior management team, and the business.

We drove hard and there were "casualties" that chose not to go on the journey – only one person, fortunately.

Fast forward a year and the results were astounding.

The company decided to put itself forward for a 'Dynamic Growth' Award that was assessed on:

> "Highlighting businesses demonstrating true growth and innovation with the energy and passion for delivering change, while including ambition to develop their workforces and to maximise technological, commercial, and M&A opportunities."

Not only did they enter but they won, with the judges explaining their decision as such:

"This company was chosen as our winner because the judges were impressed with the extraordinary growth of this business, which has reached a market position at the forefront of its sector. The company continues to pave the way, using cutting-edge technology including CO, lasers, and D3 printers, and has a coveted its place as a supplier to the Royal Navy."

In the words of Lloyd Bates, MD of Aish Technologies Ltd:

"In the past few years we have grown from £14.2 million to £18.7 million last year, 30% growth, and this year we should do £21.5 million, another 13% growth.

"Our success is brought about by our people. We put a lot of effort into the development of our people and employee engagement, getting them to understand the journey we are on, our aspirations."

He highlighted a clear vision, clear objectives, communicated regularly by briefings and newsletters, keeping everyone up-to-date with progress on the journey.

He went on to say:

"You can put a plan in place but without employee commitment you won't achieve it.

"If you can deliver what you are good at, then you can grow organically, which we have done."

Aish Technologies also won the Lloyds Bank small to medium-sized business of the year award. This award celebrates the contribution of small- and medium-sized enterprises to the UK economy, and those businesses who have maintained a consistent and strong financial performance, understood their customers, and who had an engaged workforce with effective leadership, with continual innovation to support future growth.

Creating an engaged workforce and effective leadership were critical to their success, enabling increased turnover and profitability and proved one critical point: when people—both leaders and employees—are happier and more satisfied, the quality of their work and lives dramatically improve as a result of such initiatives.

As a result of these early wins with companies, I was commissioned by the publisher Routeledge to co-author a book entitled *Mapping Motivation for Engagement* with my good friend James Sale, the world's leading expert in motivation.

Left to right: James Sale, Warren Munson, and myself, at the launch for Mapping Motivation for Engagement.

It has also paved the way to be invited to present a two-day Employee Engagement Masterclass for businesses from around the globe in the backdrop of Dubai and Kuala Lumper.

I now enjoy the privilege of working with some truly great businesses that see their employees as central to their success.

Lloyd Bates and myself at the award ceremony.
Congratulations to Aish Technologies!

"IF YOU WANT TO EARN MORE MONEY TELL A BETTER STORY."

CHAPTER 1
UNVEILING YOUR
BUSINESS ODYSSEY

Q 1. Does your company have a have a story about where it's been, where it is now and where it's going in the future?

In the world of business, where strategies are crafted meticulously and executed with precision, there exists a hidden power that often gets overlooked – the power of storytelling. As I once stated during a seminar, "If you want to earn more money, tell a better story." In the words of Peter Drucker: "Culture eats strategy for breakfast."

Imagine a workplace where every individual is driven by a common belief, a shared passion for making a significant impact on the world. This is the result of a culture, a story that binds everyone together. It goes beyond the strategic plans set by management; it delves into the soul of why the business exists. It's a story about where the business has been, where it stands now, and the future it aspires to create.

Let's contrast this with a scenario where strategy is defined by management, and there's no buy-in from the team. In this case, no story unites them, and the lack of a common purpose hinders the execution of even the most well-thought-out strategies. Here, strategy alone is insufficient: culture, the story, must come first.

To illustrate the power of culture and strategy alignment, let's delve into the tale of the Wright Brothers, pioneers of man-made flight. In the early 1900s, Wilbur and Orville Wright embarked on a journey fuelled by an unwavering passion to achieve what seemed impossible. They knew that if they could figure out man-powered flight they would change the world forever. In their own words, "What one man can do himself directly is but little. If however he can stir up ten others to take up the task he has accomplished much." Inspiring others to believe in making the impossible possible is what carried them through. They faced countless failures, financial constraints, and setbacks, yet their culture of belief propelled them forward. On December 17th, 1903, at Kitty Hawk, North Carolina, they triumphed, and man achieved flight for the first time. Their story, their culture, and their strategy were in perfect harmony.

Contrast this with Samuel Pierrepoint Langley, who was commissioned by the government of the day to work on man-powered flight. Despite being well-funded and supported, he failed to achieve the same goal. His motivation was solely driven by strategy, lacking the culture and belief that defined the Wright Brothers' success.

The lesson is clear – your story matters. Every business owner starts with a dream, a passion that forms the foundation of their story. Yet, as businesses grow, the story often gets buried, forgotten, or left untold. This oversight is a missed opportunity to stand out from the crowd.

These two examples come from a brilliant TEDTalk by Simon Sinek called 'The Golden Circle.' I highly recommend you find and watch this on YouTube. His book, *Start With Why,* is also well worth reading.

Take a moment to reflect on your business story. Why did you start it? How did it evolve? Where is it heading? Your story is not just a narrative; it's your unique point of difference in a sea of competitors. It's the reason why clients connect with you beyond the products or services you offer. Don't be a "me too" company, be a "go to" company!

As a business coach and trainer, I've experienced the transformative power of telling a compelling story first-hand. It's not just about what you do; it's about why and how you do it. Your story shapes the perception of your brand.

I liken it to the story of the silver tray and its perceived value. Think of the tray's price if bought in a car boot sale, as opposed to a High Street, as opposed to pride of place in Harrods. The value of your business, just like the silver tray, is determined by the perception created around it.

Here are three top tips to help you tell your story effectively:

Top Tip 1: Make Your Story Serve You When crafting your story, ensure that it serves your purpose. Dig deep into your journey and highlight aspects that set you apart. Remember, a better story leads to more significant rewards.

Top Tip 2: Bring Your Story to Life Through Film Capture your story on film and use it as a feature as your company grows. Share it on your website, during inductions, and in the onboarding processes, including client interactions. Visual storytelling leaves a lasting impression.

Top Tip 3: Discover Your Value through Others If you're unsure about the value you bring or your story, ask your clients and peers. Their perspective might surprise you, revealing aspects of your business that you hadn't considered. Use their insights to build a story that resonates.

In the world of business, if you're not telling your story, it will be told for you. Take control of your narrative, create the right perception, and let your story be the driving force that sets you apart on your business journey.

Tell your story, and people will listen!

"COMPANIES WITH UNUSUALLY CLEAR VISIONS OUTPERFORM THEIR COMPETITORS BY A FACTOR OF TEN."

CHAPTER 2
PAINTING THE FUTURE: THE POWER OF A THREE-YEAR VISION

Q 2. Does your company have a 3-year vision?

Nancy Reagan, Gandhi, and two diligent workers laid the foundation for understanding the transformative force of a vision.

When Ronald Reagan visited Nancy's hometown, they came across one of her ex-boyfriends. As they were leaving, Ronald commented that had she married him she would have been the wife of a real estate agent. Nancy quickly riposted that had she married him, he would have been the future president.

When Ghandi was asked for a message for his people by a reporter, he responded, "My life is my message"- what is *your* message?

When two workers were asked what they were working on, the first replied, "I'm laying Railway Tracks." The second responded, "I'm building a railway." The second saw beyond laying tracks to building a national railway and all the good it would do to help his country, his people, and organisations to thrive.

When Euro Disney was built, one of Walt Disney's Sons was interviewed by a reporter who commented on what a shame it was that Walt Disney was not there to see the theme park. Walt Disney's son replied: "He saw it 25 years ago."

They all recognised the significance of having a story and a vision.

THE VISION ADVANTAGE

In the business world, a company's three-year vision is not just a strategic plan: it's a magnetic force that attracts and retains top talent. Harvard Business School's assertion that companies with unusually clear visions outperform competitors by a factor of ten underscores the importance of having a well-defined path for the future.

How does this impact on attracting and keeping talent?

Potential or existing employees see a job offer not just as a position that pays bills, but as an opportunity to be part of something larger than themselves.

A three-year vision serves as a roadmap, offering a sense of direction and purpose to existing and potential employees. A reason to stick around or join. It conveys stability and a forward-thinking mindset, making the company a compelling prospect for potential employees.

ALIGNING ASPIRATIONS

Most Talented professionals seek more than financial compensation; they yearn for opportunities to make a meaningful impact. A three-year vision aligns the company's objectives with the aspirations of its employees. It provides a clear picture of how individual skills and efforts contribute to the company's long-term strategy, creating a sense of purpose and fulfilment.

SHOWCASING GROWTH POTENTIAL

A well-defined vision allows a company to showcase its growth potential and future opportunities. It's not just about the present; it's about the journey ahead. A company with a clear vision can articulate its growth plans, demonstrating a commitment to investing in the professional development of its employees. This foresight becomes a powerful attractor for those seeking opportunities for advancement, learning, and career development.

FOSTERING LOYALTY AND ENGAGEMENT

Retaining talent is as crucial as attracting it. Employees thrive when they see a future for themselves and understand their role in achieving the company's long-term goals. A three-year vision fosters a sense of ownership and loyalty. Employees who are aware of their contributions to the bigger picture become more engaged, satisfied, and committed to staying with the company for the long haul.

In summary, a company's three-year vision is not just a strategic document, it's a dynamic force that attracts, engages, and retains top talent. It provides a sense of purpose, aligns individual aspirations with business goals, showcases growth opportunities, and fosters loyalty.

As you embark on creating or refining your company's vision, remember: vision without action is a daydream, and action without vision is a nightmare. The true power lies in harmonising both to paint a compelling and achievable future for your business.

Top Tip 1: Clarity of Purpose Clearly define the company's vision and long-term goals. Ensure that every member of the organisation understands and aligns with the overarching vision. A succinct and compelling vision statement can serve as a guiding beacon for strategic decisions and actions.

Top Tip 2: Strategic Roadmap Develop a comprehensive strategic roadmap that outlines key milestones, targets, and initiatives over the next three years. This roadmap should address market trends, competitive analysis, and technological advancements, ensuring adaptability to changes in the business environment.

Top Tip 3: Engage Stakeholders Involve key stakeholders, including employees, customers, and investors, in the vision-setting process. Seek input and feedback to create a shared sense of ownership and commitment. Regularly communicate progress toward the vision to maintain transparency and motivation throughout the organisation.

This team is working on their 3-year organisational vision.

"EFFECTIVELY COMMUNICATING YOUR COMPANY'S VISION AND STORY IS THE KEY TO BUILDING A CONNECTION WITH YOUR AUDIENCE. IT TRANSFORMS YOUR MISSION INTO A SHARED PURPOSE, TURNING STAKEHOLDERS INTO ADVOCATES AND CUSTOMERS INTO LOYAL SUPPORTERS."

CHAPTER 3
TOTAL COMMUNICATION

Q **3. Is that story and vision totally communicated throughout the business?**

In the heart of every successful organisation lies a compelling story and a visionary outlook that permeates its very essence. The significance of effectively communicating this narrative cannot be overstated, as it serves as the lifeblood that courses through the veins of company culture, talent acquisition, talent retention, collaboration, and customer loyalty.

BUILDING A STRONG COMPANY CULTURE

Picture a workplace where every employee is not just a cog in the machine but aware of their integral part of a larger purpose. Communicating the story and vision of a business lays the foundation for a robust company culture. When the workforce comprehends the organisation's purpose, values, and long-term goals, a sense of belonging and alignment blossoms. This shared purpose becomes the driving force behind a positive work environment, fostering high morale and heightened employee engagement.

ATTRACTING TOP TALENT

Talented individuals seek more than a paycheck; they seek meaning and purpose in their work. A clear and compelling business story, coupled with a well-communicated vision, acts as a magnet for top-tier talent. Individuals are drawn to companies with narratives that resonate with their values and aspirations. They yearn to contribute to an organisation that transcends profit-making and aligns with a broader purpose.

RETAINING TALENT

The story of a business isn't just for recruitment; it's a powerful tool for talent retention. Effective communication of the company's story and vision plays a pivotal role in keeping employees motivated and satisfied. When individuals understand how their contributions contribute to the overarching vision, job satisfaction soars, and loyalty solidifies. It's the glue that binds employees to the organisation, reducing turnover and nurturing a sense of commitment.

ALIGNMENT AND COLLABORATION

In the well-orchestrated symphony of a successful business, alignment is key. Effective communication of the business story and vision creates a shared understanding that permeates the entire organisation. This shared vision becomes the catalyst for collaboration, teamwork, and a unified effort towards common goals. Employees connected to the organisation's story are more likely to work cohesively, driving productivity and fostering an environment ripe for innovation.

BRAND REPUTATION AND CUSTOMER LOYALTY

Beyond the walls of the organisation, the communicated story and vision become the public face of the brand. Businesses that effectively share their narrative with customers build a strong brand reputation and cultivate customer loyalty. When customers identify with a company's values and purpose, a long-term relationship is forged. Positive word-of-mouth referrals become commonplace, and sustainable business growth becomes an organic by-product.

In conclusion, the effective communication of a business's story and vision is the linchpin for success. It's the catalyst for building a robust company culture, attracting, and retaining top talent, fostering collaboration, and cultivating customer loyalty. In the grand tapestry of business, the story and vision are not just words; they are the vibrant threads weaving together a narrative of purpose, growth, and success.

Top Tip 1: Hear From The Founder Video the founder telling the organisation's story and vision. Return to it frequently as a reminder and use it repeatedly in communications.

Top Tip 2: Onboard The Right Way Tell your story and communicate your vision in your inductions and onboarding to make sure that right from the get-go employees understand the organisation's narrative.

Top Tip 3: Use Your Website Tell your story and communicate your vision on your website, intranet, marketing materials—wherever you can!

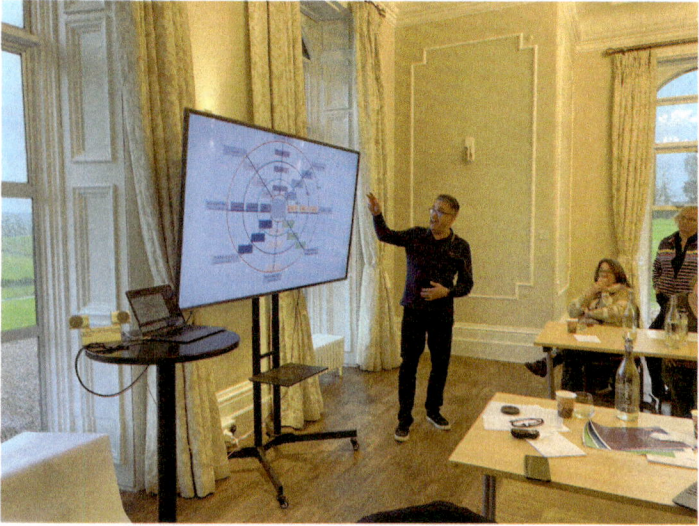

The leader of a five-venue leisure-centre business, communicating their story and vision through every level of the organisation.

"INTEGRATING YOUR COMPANY'S VISION AND STORY INTO THE INDUCTION PROCESS IS NOT JUST A FORMALITY; IT'S THE FOUNDATIONAL STEP TOWARD ALIGNING EVERY MEMBER WITH THE HEART AND SOUL OF THE ORGANISATION."

CHAPTER 4
THE POWER OF SHARED NARRATIVES

Q 4. **Do all employees know it, is it part of your induction, do your customers know it?**

In the ever-evolving landscape of business, communication isn't just about exchanging information, it's about shaping narratives that resonate within the hearts and minds of those within and beyond the organisation. The importance of effectively communicating a business's story and vision cannot be overstated, as it serves as the linchpin for various aspects that drive organisational success.

BUILDING A STRONG COMPANY CULTURE

The story and vision of a business are the foundational elements upon which a robust company culture is built. When the purpose, values, and long-term goals are clearly communicated, employees gain a profound understanding of the organisation's identity. This understanding fosters a sense of belonging and alignment, transforming the workplace into a community bound by a shared sense of purpose. The result is a positive work environment that not only boosts employee morale but also significantly enhances overall employee engagement.

ATTRACTING TOP TALENT

In the competitive talent landscape, a clear and compelling story, coupled with a well-communicated vision, acts as a powerful magnet. Top-tier professionals are drawn to companies that transcend the mundane, offering a narrative that aligns with their personal values and aspirations. Beyond the allure of salary packages, individuals seek an organisation that provides a purpose beyond profit-making – an environment where their professional journey is intertwined with a broader, more meaningful story.

Attracting and retaining top talent is a critical priority for businesses. According to McKinsey, superior talent can be up to eight times more productive, and high performers are 400-800 percent more productive than average ones! Just let that sink in.

When companies emphasise their story and vision, it helps differentiate them in the talent market. Potential employees who resonate with the company's purpose and vision are more likely to be attracted to, and apply for, job opportunities. In addition, employees who align with the organisation's story and vision are more likely to stay with the organisation long term, reducing turnover and associated costs.

RETAINING TALENT

Effective communication of the business's story and vision isn't just a recruitment strategy—it's a cornerstone of talent retention. When the link between individual contributions and the overarching vision is crystal clear, employees see the impact of their work, fostering a deeper job satisfaction that translates into loyalty. In addition, when employees work in line with their values (and motivations), their energy levels and hence productivity increase. Clear communication reduces turnover, creating a workforce committed to the long-term success of the organisation.

ALIGNMENT AND COLLABORATION

Within the organisation, a shared understanding and alignment are catalysts for collaboration and teamwork. The story and vision act as a common language, creating a unified effort towards achieving common goals. Employees who feel connected to the organisation's narrative are more likely to work together cohesively. The result is not just improved productivity but also a breeding ground for innovation. When teams share a vision, diverse talents converge to create a dynamic synergy that propels the organisation towards success.

BRAND REPUTATION AND CUSTOMER LOYALTY

Beyond the office walls, the external communication of a business's story and vision shapes its brand reputation. Customers today seek more than just products or services: they seek a connection with the values and purpose of the brands they choose. Effective communication builds a bridge between the organisation and its customers, fostering a relationship beyond the transactional. A business that resonates with its customers on a deeper level not only builds a strong brand reputation but also cultivates customer loyalty.

In summary, the effective communication of a business's story and vision is a multifaceted solution that influences internal dynamics and external perceptions. It forms the bedrock of a strong company culture, attracts top talent, retains a motivated workforce, promotes alignment and collaboration, and contributes significantly to building a positive brand reputation. As organisations navigate the complexities of the business world, the power of shared narratives emerges as a strategic imperative, shaping the trajectory of success.

> **Top Tip 1: Spread The Word** As we've established, not only should your employees know about your story and vision, but your customers too. Talk about your story and your vision with clients and potential clients. Include it in your sales process and when you talk about "Why use us". Put it in proposals.

> **Top Tip 2: Feedback Is The Breakfast of Champions** These wise words from Ken Blanchard are words to live by! And remember, feedback is not just about criticism or pointing out where things can be improved. Let your employees know when their actions have directly contributed to the shared narrative.

> **Top Tip 3: Make It Visual** How can your story be incorporated into your brand identity? How can your logo or design aesthetics embody your organisation's cultural narrative? This way, the story really is running through every facet of the business, and there as a reminder on every letterhead.

A successful training day, working with people from all levels of the business.

AS MAYA ANGELOU WISELY SAID, "PEOPLE WILL FORGET WHAT YOU SAID, PEOPLE WILL FORGET WHAT YOU DID, BUT PEOPLE WILL NEVER FORGET HOW YOU MADE THEM FEEL."

CHAPTER 5
ENGAGING LEADERS &
MANAGERS

Q 5: Do you have engaging managers and leaders across the business?

There is saying: employees don't quit their jobs, they quit their managers. Over the years, this has proven to be truer and truer, and I'm sure this resonates with many reading this.

In my opinion, poor leadership and management have probably been the biggest cause of loss of talent in recent years. It has also probably been the biggest major contributor to inconsistency of productivity and growth; these are a direct result of inconsistent leadership and management across an organisation. We all personally know people we consider to be good or bad leaders. And most of us have witnessed firsthand the impact of good or bad leadership. Inconsistency in leadership and management leads to varied performance and thus inconsistent productivity levels.

Why is this? It is simple really: in my experience, most managers and leaders end up in these roles by default. It's a natural way someone progresses in an organisation. However, how many great technically gifted individuals simply struggle to perform well at management level? Think of the great salesperson who is promoted to team leader – despite the fact it's the last thing they want – but peer pressure dictates they take the role. Do they succeed? Invariably not. We must think about "fit for purpose" and if they are rightly upskilled and trained.

Every day, individuals are promoted into leadership and management positions with no training; they sink or swim based on past experiences. But the real is issue is that if they sink, all the employees they're responsible for sink as well.

Having engaging managers and leaders across the business is therefore crucial for attracting and keeping talent. These individuals play a pivotal role in creating a positive and motivating work environment, which directly impacts employees' satisfaction, productivity, and commitment to the organisation.

What are the properties of an engaging manager or leader?

Firstly, engaging managers and leaders have the ability to inspire and motivate their teams. They possess excellent communication skills and are adept at articulating a compelling vision and goals for the organisation. When employees feel connected to a larger purpose and understand how their contributions align with the company's objectives, they are more likely to be engaged and motivated to perform at their best.

Secondly, engaging managers and leaders foster a culture of trust and open communication. They actively listen to their employees' concerns, provide regular feedback, and encourage collaboration and innovation. By creating a supportive and inclusive work environment, these leaders establish strong relationships with their team members, promoting loyalty and a sense of belonging.

Furthermore, engaging managers and leaders prioritise the development and growth of their employees. They invest in training and mentorship programmes, provide opportunities for skill enhancement, and recognise and reward achievements. Such initiatives demonstrate a genuine commitment to employees' professional advancement, which increases their satisfaction and encourages them to stay with the organisation for the long term.

The presence of engaging managers and leaders also enhances the employer brand and reputation. Positive word-of-mouth from satisfied employees can attract top talent to the organisation. Consider this – you are only as good as what your worst employee says about you! When potential candidates see that the company values its employees, provides opportunities for growth, and fosters a positive work environment, they are more likely to be attracted to join and contribute their skills and expertise.

In conclusion, having engaging managers and leaders throughout the business is essential for attracting and retaining talent. Their ability to inspire, build trust, prioritise employee development, and enhance the overall work environment significantly impacts employee satisfaction and commitment. Ultimately, organisations that prioritise engaging leadership are better positioned to attract top talent and create a culture that fosters long-term employee retention.

So, what skills do these managers and leaders need? Here are just a few.

1. The right Mindset to both challenge and support employees
2. The ability to be flexible in their style to accommodate employees at different levels of development.
3. The ability to build trust.

4. Understanding how to Coach & Mentor.
5. The ability to set strategic direction and create breakthrough plans.
6. Ongoing two-way appraisal and management by walking about, not hiding.

Top Tip 1: Train The Trainers Provide leadership and management training on a consistent and ongoing basis.

Top Tip 2: Develop Coaches Ensure leaders and managers have coaching skills and can run ongoing appraisals, which are two way.

Top Tip 3: Envision Ensure leaders and managers know how to set the vision and strategic direction for the business and/or their teams.

The importance of good leaders cannot be overstated!

"MOTIVATION IS LIKE BATHING; IT NEEDS TO BE DONE DAILY."

CHAPTER 6
THE STRATEGIC IMPERATIVE OF DAILY COACHING

Q 6. Do those managers coach, stretch and motivate employees daily?

The Strategic Imperative of Daily Coaching

In the ever-evolving landscape of business, where the competition for top talent is fiercer than ever, the role of leaders and managers transcends traditional directives.

Today, the true measure of a leader's success lies not only in meeting targets and achieving goals but in the daily commitment to coaching, stretching, and motivating employees.

Why, you might ask, is this a strategic imperative in the modern workplace?

EMPOWERING THROUGH COACHING

Coaching-oriented leaders understand that their own success is intricately tied to the success of those they lead. Rather than wielding authority as a blunt instrument, they recognise the importance of empowerment.

By adopting a coaching mindset, leaders create an environment where each employee feels valued, acknowledged, and motivated. This empowerment not only boosts individual well-being but also propels overall performance to new heights.

In an era where the value of collaboration and innovation is paramount, the ability to cultivate a team that thinks outside the box and solves problems collectively is a competitive advantage that sets successful organisations apart.

BUILDING TRUST THROUGH RELATIONSHIPS

Leaders who coach do more than manage; they build relationships. In the age of remote work and digital communication, the personal touch often gets lost in the virtual shuffle.

Coaching-oriented leaders invest time in understanding the nuances of their team members' lives, aspirations, and challenges. This investment in relationships goes beyond a superficial understanding; it builds trust.

Remember, we are no longer in the game of "managing the employee"; we are now responsible for the person.

Employees who trust their leaders are more likely to stay committed to the organisation. The foundation of this loyalty is laid by leaders who genuinely care about the well-being and professional success of their team. This is not just about meeting targets but about creating an environment where individuals feel seen, heard, and supported.

FOSTERING CONTINUOUS GROWTH

In a world where the only constant is change, the ability to adapt and grow is a skill that is prised above all.

Coaching-oriented leaders recognise this and actively contribute to the growth and development of their team members. They don't simply provide answers: they ask the right questions.

These leaders understand the importance of encouraging critical thinking, generating innovative solutions, and continually developing skills and capabilities. The culture of continuous learning and improvement that stems from this approach is a magnet for talented individuals seeking personal and professional development opportunities.

We are in an era where smart leaders and managers get out of the way, not in the way, of the contributions of teams, individuals, and talented employees.

NAVIGATING THE GREAT RESIGNATION

In the face of unprecedented challenges like the Great Resignation, where employees are reevaluating their professional paths and seeking meaning in their work, leaders who coach become anchors.

By providing ongoing support, guidance, and constructive feedback, they create an environment where employees not only feel motivated but also engaged with the organisation's purpose.

The alignment of personal goals and aspirations with the greater purpose of the organisation instils a sense of meaning and belonging. This sense of purpose becomes a powerful force in talent retention, especially during turbulent times when employees are contemplating their professional journey.

One of the things I've introduced to my clients is a platform that allows managers and leaders to understand what motivates their people, teams, and organisation.

This platform enables managers and leaders to understand how to describe, measure, monitor, and maximise motivation with individuals, teams and the overall business.

There are nine key work motivators, and we have all of them to a lesser or greater extent.

The key is to identify the more prominent ones and assess how much the organisation is harnessing them or not.

We want people to "want to" not "have to" come to work and if we can achieve this we will get that discretionary effort, willingly.

It is so powerful it underpins everything I do with my clients.

It is powerful because unlike personality, motivation is dynamic and changeable beast.

A simple strategic decision can have a massive impact on whether someone leaves or stays and by understanding an employee's motivation we can address any negative impact immediately.

Equally, by understanding individual and team motivations we can make strategic decisions on how to harness their motivations for the benefit of those individuals and teams, as well as the entire organisation.

We can also track motivational trends to identify opportunities to accelerate growth for individuals, teams, and the overall organisation.

I was working with a client, they had 170 employees. We mapped everyone's motivations, and we identified 5 key individuals that were at risk of leaving because their motivations were not being met.

To the outside world—their colleagues and the business—it was not evident that they were demotivated because they were still performing to a standard, which is testament to their professionalism, but inside they were losing the will to live.

They were most probably working with sheer resilience, which if left unaddressed could have led to ill health, sickness and/or loss of talent.

We've all seen this scenario before, where a key member of a team resigns unexpectedly, leaving a real hole to fill and a challenge for the organisation.

Fortunately, my client personally sat down with all 5 individually and re-engaged them in the business—now *that* is real leadership!

He told me later that he estimated retaining these 5 employees saved him over a million pounds in lost productivity, recruitment, and the key clients they could have taken with them.

Unfortunately, this unseen loss of motivation is happening more and more with the Great Resignation. Spotting it early and addressing it, like my client did, therefore becomes paramount to continued success and talent retention.

Now a lot of businesses do a 90-day appraisal of their business KPIs.

My question is: why are they not doing it for their second most expensive item after their capital investment—their people?

For me, it is a no brainer.

It is so important my clients undertake a motivational appraisal of their people every 90 days, as it not only unlocks motivation, but it also harnesses it for the good of all and identifies any threats to loss of talent.

Leaders and managers who commit to coaching, stretching, and motivating employees daily are not merely contributing to the success of their teams—they are shaping the future of their organisations.

Their strategic approach to leadership fosters not only individual development but also strengthens relationships, enhances well-being and motivation, and cultivates a profound sense of purpose and belonging.

Organisations that embrace this approach are not just workplaces. They are thriving ecosystems that attract and retain the brightest talents in the ever-evolving business landscape.

> **Top Tip 1: Get Motivated!** Introduce a 90-Day Motivation Action Plan for employees (contact me to find the best solution).

> **Top Tip 2: Ongoing Motivational Appraisal** Motivation is not a "one and done" thing. Real motivation is a continuous journey. Ensure leaders and managers have the coaching skills to run a motivational ongoing appraisals process, which are two-way.

> **Top Tip 3: Hire Based On Attitude Not Skills** Skills can be taught, but motivation—what drives us—is far more difficult to change. Recruit the right managers and leaders with the right attitudes and behaviours.

At one of our training days, two leaders learned the power of one to one coaching.

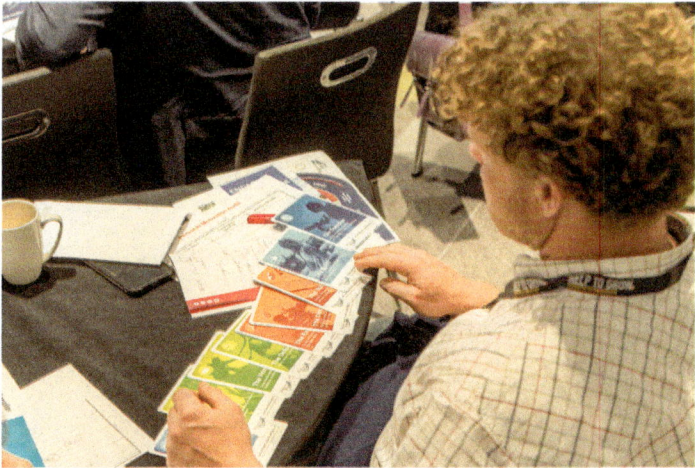

What motivates you? This is a good preliminary exercise before taking the actual diagnostic.

RICHARD BRANSON WILL TELL YOU HE EMPLOYS PEOPLE SO THAT THEY CAN TELL HIM WHAT TO DO, NOT THE OTHER WAY AROUND. ARE YOU LISTENING TO YOUR TALENT?

CHAPTER 7
LISTENING CULTURES

Q **7. Do you have a listening culture?**
I see a lot of companies employ fantastic talent only to turn around and bombard them with "messages" rather than harness the thoughts and ideas of the talent they have recruited. This seems criminal to me.

It was Richard Branson who said that he employs talented individuals so they can tell him what to do. How refreshing and obvious. Surrounding yourself with talent only works if you harness the thoughts and ideas of these talented individuals.

In the symphony of business, the notes of success are often played by the skilled hands of talented individuals.

Attracting and retaining such talent has become a pursuit as competitive as any sport.

To stand out in this dynamic landscape, businesses must embrace a fundamental shift—the cultivation of a listening culture.

TUNING INTO THE WORKFORCE

The question that should echo through the corridors of every organisation: Do you have a listening culture?

In an era where the demands and expectations of the workforce are evolving at an unprecedented pace, relying on traditional methods to understand employee sentiment is akin to playing yesterday's number one hit in a world demanding new songs.

Annual surveys, once the de facto method of gauging employee morale, now fall short in capturing the nuances of contemporary workplace dynamics.

Enter the era of continuous listening, fortified by the power of people analytics. When your employees stop talking to you it's too late!

This strategy not only monitors the heartbeat of an organisation in real-time but also nurtures an ongoing dialogue with employees.

This is the essence of a listening culture.

THE HARMONY OF TRUST, PARTNERSHIP, AND OPEN COMMUNICATION

Trust, like a delicate thread, can be easily broken.

A listening culture, however, weaves a tapestry of trust, partnership, and open communication.

It is a catalyst for the creation of a positive work environment, where employees are not only heard but truly understood.

This understanding fosters engagement, satisfaction, and commitment – the key elements in the composition of a successful workplace.

Beyond the immediate benefits, a listening culture positions organisations as keen observers of the ever-changing workplace landscape.

It enables them to identify emerging trends, seize opportunities, and proactively address issues before they cascade into major discord.

THE MAGNETISM OF LISTENING

The allure of a listening culture is magnetic, especially for top performers.

Talented individuals are drawn to organisations that not only value their opinions but implement their suggestions, organisations that provide avenues for continuous growth and prioritise employee well-being.

When the workplace becomes a stage where every voice matters, employees become not just participants but active contributors to the success.

In the competitive talent market, where the war for skilled individuals rages on, a listening culture draws the best of the best like a banner.

AN ANTHEM OF COMMITMENT

In the end, a listening culture is an anthem of commitment that has everyone singing "from the same hymn sheet". It is a commitment to creating an environment that values individual contributions and fosters collaboration.

It is a commitment to actively listening to the needs and preferences of employees, creating a workplace where trust, engagement, and productivity flourish.

In this dynamic and competitive landscape, a listening culture is not just a desirable trait, but a vital necessity.

It attracts top talent and ensures their long-term commitment and contribution to the success of the business.

In my opinion, one of the biggest threats to growth is the inability to attract and retain talent. That is why developing a listening culture is so vital.

> **Top Tip 1: Listen Well** The sign of a poor leader/manager is when employees stop contributing. Train your leaders/managers in coaching/listening skills.
>
> **Top Tip 2: Involve Employees Early In Decision-Making** Seek their thoughts and ideas.
>
> **Top Tip 3: Seek The Best** Recruit people *better* than you and listen to what they say.

On a training day. Note the attentiveness with which the delegates are listening to one another!

CUSTOMERS WILL NEVER LOVE YOUR BUSINESS UNTIL YOUR EMPLOYEES LOVE IT FIRST. MAKING YOUR PEOPLE CENTRAL TO DECISION MAKING IS KEY TO ACHIEVING THIS.

CHAPTER 8
THE PEOPLE-CENTRIC PARADIGM: A NECESSITY FOR ORGANISATIONAL SUCCESS

Q 8. Are your people central in decision making or do you just cascade messages?

The People-Centric Paradigm: A Necessity for Organisational Success

The traditional top-down approach to decision-making is increasingly being challenged in today's business landscape.

The era of "cascading" messages down from the executive echelons to the workforce has given way to a more inclusive and participatory model.

The question now is: Are your people central in decision-making, or are decisions merely cascaded down through the organisational hierarchy?

In today's fast-paced and dynamic business environment, the role of employees in the decision-making process is not just a tick-box exercise in winning moral brownie points, but a critical necessity.

The benefits of transitioning towards a people-centric approach are profound and extend far beyond the confines of strategy.

Let's delve into why involving individuals in decision-making is imperative for organisational success.

EMPOWERMENT AND ENGAGEMENT

When employees become active participants in decision-making processes, a profound transformation occurs in their relationship with their work.

The sense of empowerment and ownership that arises from contributing to decisions fosters a deeper engagement. This heightened engagement is a catalyst for increased job satisfaction, motivation, and commitment to the organisation. The knock on effect of this is an increase in productivity and bottom line too.

Think about it: if they are coming up with the ideas as individuals and teams, then they are bought into the outcome and ultimate success by default.

The feeling of being valued and appreciated translates into a powerful loyalty, strengthening the bond between the employee and the company.

DIVERSE PERSPECTIVES AND INNOVATION

A diverse team brings a multitude of perspectives, experiences, and ideas to the decision-making table.

Inclusion of voices from different backgrounds and areas of expertise sparks creativity and innovation.

The synergy of diverse minds results in collective intelligence that surpasses individual capabilities.

This diversity-driven innovation becomes a potent force for effective problem-solving and the ability to adapt to the ever-changing dynamics of the market.

AGILITY AND ADAPTABILITY

In an era where agility is synonymous with competitiveness, organisations must be able to pivot swiftly in response to market changes. This was never more true than since the pandemic which, bizarrely, illustrated the speed of innovation and adopting new ways of working.

The frontline knowledge and insights possessed by employees become invaluable in this context. To use a military analogy, it is your front-line soldiers who are actually *in* the trenches and can provide you with accurate data about what is going on.

By involving employees in decision-making, organisations tap into a wealth of real-time information.

This not only expedites the decision-making process but also allows for quicker adaptation without being bogged down by cumbersome hierarchical approval procedures.

A culture of agility is born from involving employees in every level of the decision-making processes, ensuring the organisation's readiness to anticipate, and be proactive in engaging with, the challenges of the fast-paced business world.

TALENT ATTRACTION AND RETENTION

Attracting and retaining top talent is a perpetual challenge for organisations aiming for sustained success.

A people-centric approach to decision-making becomes a key differentiator in this quest.

Potential employees are drawn to environments that recognise and value their contributions.

The assurance of a workplace that encourages growth and development, where ideas are heard and considered, is a compelling factor for talent attraction.

Moreover, once within the organisation, employees are more likely to stay when they feel their voices matter and are integral to the decision-making fabric of the company.

In summary, the shift towards a people-centric paradigm in decision-making is not merely a strategic choice: it is an investment in the core strength of any organisation – its people.

This shift empowers individuals, cultivates a culture of collaboration, fuels innovation, promotes agility, and fosters inclusivity.

The ripple effects extend to talent attraction and retention, ultimately contributing to the long-term success and sustainability of the organisation both in times of turbulence and abundance.

Top Tip 1: Foster Inclusive Decision-Making Actively involve your team members in decision-making processes. Create a culture that values diverse perspectives and encourages open communication. Consider implementing regular brainstorming sessions, team meetings, or collaborative workshops to gather input before making decisions.

Top Tip 2: Empower and Delegate Responsibility Instead of merely cascading messages, empower your team by delegating decision-making authority. Provide individuals with the autonomy to make choices within their areas of expertise. This creates a sense of ownership and accountability.

Top Tip 3: Communicate Transparently Establish clear communication channels that facilitate transparency in decision-making processes. Ensure that everyone understands the rationale behind decisions and the impact on the team or organisation. Whether the decision is made centrally or collaboratively, keeping everyone informed and involved enhances overall team cohesion.

Involve people in every level of decision-making to achieve buy-in.

"EMBRACING A SHARED SET OF VALUES AMONG EMPLOYEES IS THE CORNERSTONE OF ORGANISATIONAL SUCCESS, DRIVING PERFORMANCE AND ATTRACTING INDIVIDUALS WHO RESONATE WITH YOUR VISION."

CHAPTER 9
THE PILLARS OF PURPOSE

Q **9. Do you have a set of values?**

In this era, where financial compensation is no longer the sole motivator for individuals seeking professional fulfilment, the significance of a company's values has emerged as a decisive factor in attracting and retaining top-tier talent.

Employees are now driven by a desire to align their personal beliefs with the ethos of their workplace.

Thus, an organisation's set of values is not just a mere statement on paper; it is the bedrock upon which a thriving and sustainable business stands, and upon which potential and existing employees make career decisions.

Why does it matter?

Companies that articulate and embody a clear set of values set themselves apart from the competition.

This is not merely a matter of rhetoric: it's about creating an environment that resonates with the aspirations and principles of its workforce.

A well-defined set of values serves as a North Star, guiding employees through the wilderness of daily tasks towards a shared purpose.

Imagine a prospective employee evaluating job offers.

Amidst the sea of opportunities, the companies that shine brightest are those with a robust value system.

It becomes a lens through which job seekers can decipher what truly matters to an organisation, how they will be treated, and what kind of culture they will be a part of.

For instance, a company prioritising customer service or sustainability is likely to attract individuals who seek a profound sense of purpose in their work.

These individuals are drawn to organisations where their efforts transcend the mundane and contribute to something larger than themselves.

The statistics echo the growing importance of values in the eyes of professionals globally.

According to a study conducted by LinkedIn, in Europe, 59% of respondents expressed a reluctance to work for an organisation that does not share their values, even if enticed with a higher salary.

In the UK, France, Germany, and Ireland, a staggering 68% of workers prioritise organisations aligned with their values.

Crossing the Atlantic, the trend intensifies with 87% of American workers and 85% of Brazilian workers seeking workplaces that echo their core beliefs.

This trend is particularly conspicuous among the younger generations, who exhibit a remarkable willingness to pivot careers in pursuit of organisations that mirror their values.

Be it environmental sustainability, ethical business practices, or a commitment to social responsibility, the millennial and Gen Z workforce is reshaping the professional landscape.

The bottom line is clear: a company's set of values is not an ornamental accessory; it is the lifeblood of a thriving, resilient, and forward-thinking organisation.

It is the invisible force that attracts, retains, and fuels the dynamic engine of talent in the competitive arena of the modern job market.

As we navigate the complexities of contemporary business, remember, the pillars of purpose are not just a luxury – they are a necessity.

> **Top Tip 1: Alignment with Mission** Ensure that your business values align with the overall mission and purpose of your company. When values are congruent with your mission, they become a powerful guide for decision-making and behaviour, creating a cohesive and purpose-driven organisational culture.
>
> **Top Tip 2: Employee Involvement** Involve employees in the process of setting values. Solicit their input and feedback to create a sense of ownership and commitment. Values that reflect the shared beliefs and aspirations of your team are more likely to be embraced and practiced throughout the organisation.
>
> **Top Tip 3: Practical and Observable** Craft values that are practical and observable in everyday work. Tangible and measurable values make it easier for employees to understand and integrate them into their daily activities. This clarity helps reinforce the desired behaviours and fosters a culture that embodies the chosen values.

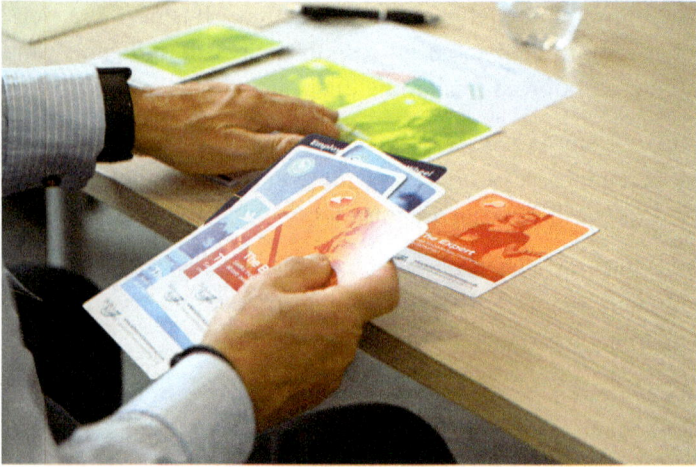

*Motivational drivers and values are linked. Do you understand your drivers
and how they create your values?*

"EMBED YOUR VALUES INTO THE DNA OF YOUR BUSINESS, AND WATCH AS CLARITY AND PURPOSE BECOME BEACONS, ATTRACTING NOT JUST EMPLOYEES AND CLIENTS, BUT KINDRED SPIRITS WHO RESONATE WITH WHAT YOU STAND FOR."

CHAPTER 10
BREATHING LIFE INTO VALUES

Q **10. Do you live and breathe your company values?**

Now, it is one thing to say you have values, but do you live and breathe them?

It has been said we live in the "post-truth" era. And yet, truth —and authenticity—is evidently a primary concern for Millennial and Gen Z employees. They will not be deceived by superficial displays. Any dissonance between espoused values and lived values will be quickly discovered and exposed as hypocrisy.

When a company embraces its values, it should not merely be a statement on a website or a plaque on the office wall.

These values become the guiding principles that inform the organisation's goals and decisions. Therefore, if we are going to involve employees in goal-setting and decision-making, as we have discussed, then we must "walk the walk" as well as talking the talk.

If social justice and equality are proclaimed as core values, they must be more than mere words; they must be backed by tangible efforts and investments, baked into the very substance of the organisation. Ask yourself this question: If an employee asked you, in an interview, what you were doing to embody your values, what would you say to them? What evidence could you show them?

And is the evidence convincing enough?

Potential recruits seek assurance that the company's commitment to social justice is not just a veneer but is deeply ingrained in the organisational DNA.

When employees witness the active embodiment of their organisation's values, it goes one step further than creating a positive work environment.

It instils a sense of belonging, fostering higher engagement and unwavering loyalty.

The commitment to values becomes a two-way street: the company invests in its employees, and in return, employees invest their dedication and skills into the company's success.

In summary, living and embodying company values is not just a tick -box in the corporate strategy.

Values provide a clear purpose, align employees with shared goals, and help potential hires assess cultural fit.

Companies that prioritise their values and back them up with tangible actions are the ones who stand out, not just as employers but as beacons of a workplace culture that transcends the quotidian.

> **Top Tip 1: Lead by Example** Demonstrate the company values in your daily actions and decisions. Your behaviour sets the tone for the organisation, and when others see you embodying the values, it encourages them to do the same.

> **Top Tip 2: Integrate Values into Processes** Infuse the company values into various aspects of the business, such as

hiring, performance evaluations, and strategic planning. This ensures that the values are not just aspirational statements but are actively considered in key business practices.

Top Tip 3: Communicate Consistently Regularly communicate and reinforce the importance of the company values through internal channels. This can include team meetings, newsletters, or recognition programmes. Consistent communication helps to keep the values at the forefront of everyone's minds, fostering a culture where they are lived and breathed daily.

Here managers celebrate their successes, understanding how motivation and values drive organisational success! (Abu Dubai)

"CLARITY IN EXPECTATIONS, COUPLED WITH MEANINGFUL CONSEQUENCES AND REWARDS ALIGNED WITH OUR VALUES, SERVES AS THE COMPASS GUIDING EMPLOYEES TOWARDS THE BEHAVIOURS WE AIM TO CULTIVATE."

CHAPTER 11
CREATING ALIGNMENT

Q **11. Are there consequences and rewards attached to the values?**

One way to live and breathe your values is to ensure that consequences and rewards are attached to these values.

Let's explore this in more detail:

ALIGNMENT OF VALUES

Consequences and rewards tied to company values help ensure accountability that employees are aligned with the organisation's mission, vision, and culture.

The strongest cultures and empires that the world has ever known, those that endured for centuries, were so long-lived because its people shared values and worked in alignment. An even more radical example might be a religion; religions are cultures of shared values and beliefs, and they have created organisations that have endured for millennia! Whether you are religious or not, the evidence is clear: groups of individuals who share values tend to (1) get a lot done and (2) survive for longer than those who don't. After all, almost every culture that did not have shared values as a foundation have been quickly swept aside and destroyed.

Alignment is essential for fostering a cohesive and unified workforce, where everyone is working towards common goals.

MOTIVATION AND RECOGNITION

By attaching consequences and rewards to company values, organisations can motivate employees to embody those values in their daily work.

When employees see that their efforts align with the company's values and are recognised and rewarded accordingly, it reinforces a positive work environment and encourages them to perform at their best.

This creates a cycle of continuous improvement, where employees are motivated to consistently contribute to the organisation's success.

Recognition can take various forms, such as monetary rewards, promotions, career development opportunities, or public appreciation.

In fact, when we look at the motivations of employees we see that there are a multitude of ways to reward them based on the different motivational drivers—either of the individual or the team.

The motivational assessment we spoke of earlier can help in ensuring that employees are rewarded in a way the aligns to their motivations, thus really reinforcing great behaviour and engaging the employee in the right way. It's worth noting here that many organisational reward schemes do not take into account the motivations or preferences of their employees, and this can mean that employees intentionally seek to *avoid* being rewarded, to avoid standing out, and avoid putting in that extra commitment and dedication.

But by understanding an employee's motivations, and rewarding them accordingly when they perform in line with the organisation's values, one kills two birds with one stone: reinforcing the organisation's commitment to their values and boosting the employee in a way they appreciate. This might be described as "virtuous circle" of improvement.

TALENT ATTRACTION

Needless to say, in a competitive job market, companies with clear and well-communicated values, along with associated consequences and rewards, have an advantage in attracting top talent.

Potential candidates who find their values resonate with the company's are more likely to be attracted to the organisation and see it as a place where they can thrive personally and professionally.

The presence of consequences and rewards tied to values demonstrates that the company takes its values seriously and creates an environment conducive to growth and success.

RETENTION AND EMPLOYEE SATISFACTION

Consequences and rewards linked to company values also contribute to employee satisfaction and retention. When employees feel recognised and rewarded for upholding the organisation's values, they are more likely to stay committed to the company for the long term.

Employees feel appreciated, supported, and motivated when they are rewarded in ways that feed their motivators and align with their values, reducing turnover rates and associated costs.

Additionally, employees who align with the company's values are more likely to find fulfilment and meaning in their work, enhancing their overall job satisfaction.

This emotional connection to the organisation not only improves retention but also positively impacts the quality of work produced and the level of dedication employees bring to their roles.

IN CONCLUSION

In conclusion, having consequences and rewards tied to company values plays a vital role in attracting and retaining talent. It sets the moral standards of the organisations.

It fosters alignment, motivation, recognition, and employee satisfaction, which collectively contribute to a strong and engaged workforce.

As organisations continue to prioritise these elements, they not only enhance their internal culture but also position themselves as the "employers of choice" in a competitive business landscape.

Top Tip 1: Align Consequences and Rewards with Values Ensure that consequences and rewards are directly tied to the specific business values you want to promote. Clearly define how adherence to or violation of each value will result in corresponding consequences or rewards. This alignment helps employees understand the direct impact of their actions on the organisation and reinforces the importance of upholding the stated values.

Top Tip 2: Transparent Communication Establish clear and transparent communication channels regarding the consequences and rewards associated with business values. Clearly communicate the expectations, consequences for non-compliance, and rewards for exemplary behaviours. This communication should be ongoing, integrated into training programmes, and readily accessible through various channels, such as employee handbooks, internal communications, and training materials.

Top Tip 3: Consistent Implementation Consistency is key in reinforcing the connection between actions and outcomes. Apply consequences and rewards consistently across all levels of the organisation to avoid perceptions of favouritism or unfair treatment. Leaders and managers should be consistent in their enforcement of consequences and recognition of positive behaviours. This consistency builds trust among employees and reinforces the organisation's commitment to its values.

Alignment of vision bridges the gap.

"INTEGRATING VALUES AND BEHAVIOURS INTO YOUR APPRAISAL PROCESS ENSURES THEY ARE NOT JUST ARTICULATED BUT LIVED, EVIDENCED, AND INGRAINED IN THE FABRIC OF YOUR BUSINESS."

CHAPTER 12
EMBEDDING COMPANY VALUES IN APPRAISAL PROCESSES

Q 12. Are they part of your appraisal process?

Not only should the organisation's values be embedded in the organisation's reward strategies, but also in their appraisal processes. Let's look at a few reasons why.

ALIGNMENT WITH ORGANISATIONAL GOALS

Company values serve as the bedrock upon which an organisation builds its identity, direction, and purpose.

When integrated into the appraisal process, they become a powerful mechanism for aligning individual actions with broader organisational objectives.

When I work with clients, values are included in a 90-day motivational appraisals process and linked naturally to motivational rewards and actions.

By evaluating and rewarding employees based on their adherence to these values, organisations ensure that every team member contributes to the common goals, fostering a cohesive and unified workforce.

The correlation between individual actions and company goals becomes palpable, creating a shared sense of purpose among employees.

Through this alignment, the appraisal process becomes a dynamic tool for steering the workforce towards a collective vision, ensuring that each individual's efforts propel the organisation forward.

Remember the story about President Kennedy visiting NASA during the 1962 space-race. President Kennedy noticed a man with a broomstick sweeping up some rubbish and asked the man what he was doing. The man replied: "I'm helping put a man on the moon, Mr. President." Though a humble janitor, the man with the broomstick had a clear sense he was part of an organisational team, and what the mission and values of that team were.

REINFORCING DESIRED BEHAVIOURS

In a world that loves numbers and data-points and percentages, it can be easy to lose the thread of our values. The appraisal process is not merely a numerical exercise; it is an opportunity to reinforce and celebrate behaviours that embody the company's core values.

By incorporating evidence of employees exemplifying these values, organisations elevate the significance of desired behaviours from abstract ideals to tangible benchmarks for success.

Recognition and acknowledgment in regular appraisal process serve as powerful motivators. Individuals who consistently demonstrate the company's values feel not only validated but inspired to continue their positive contributions.

This recognition becomes a shining light for others, setting a standard for behaviours that permeates the organisation and contributes to the creation of a values-driven work environment.

CULTURAL CONSISTENCY AND EMPLOYEE ENGAGEMENT

An organisation's values are the DNA of its culture. When employees live and breathe these values, a profound sense of belonging and purpose emerges.

Integrating evidence of employees embodying company values into the appraisal process reinforces cultural consistency, creating a strong sense of identity among the workforce.

This sense of belonging, driven by a shared commitment to the company's values, enhances employee engagement and job satisfaction.

Employees who feel connected to the organisation's purpose are more likely to invest themselves fully in their roles, resulting in improved overall organisational performance.

PERFORMANCE ENHANCEMENT

Values-based appraisal processes transcend the traditional focus on task completion. They encourage employees to align their actions with the broader ethical framework and principles of the organisation. This alignment fosters collaboration, teamwork, and ethical decision-making, ultimately leading to enhanced performance.

Employees, when aware of the impact of their actions on the organisation's success, are motivated to go beyond the mundane and strive for excellence.

Values-based appraisals thus become a catalyst for improved productivity, higher performance standards, and heightened customer satisfaction.

TALENT ACQUISITION AND RETENTION

In the competitive landscape of talent acquisition, a company's commitment to its values becomes a distinguishing factor. Organisations that incorporate values into their appraisal processes signal a genuine commitment to fostering a positive work environment.

This commitment, in turn, attracts like-minded individuals who share the same principles.

The values-centric appraisal process not only aids in acquiring top talent but also contributes significantly to employee retention.

Individuals who find alignment between their personal values and those of the organisation are more likely to stay committed and contribute to the long-term success of the company.

The evidence is compelling: integrating company values into the appraisal process is not a mere formality, it is a strategic imperative with far-reaching benefits.

It aligns individual actions with organisational goals, reinforces positive behaviours, fosters cultural consistency, enhances performance, and contributes to both talent acquisition and retention.

By emphasising the importance of company values, organisations can shape a workplace culture that not only promotes individual success but also propels the entire organisation towards enduring excellence.

The appraisal process, when infused with the essence of company values, becomes a dynamic force for cultivating a workforce that is not only proficient but also deeply aligned with the organisation's core principles.

Top Tip 1: Alignment Assessment Evaluate employee performance based on the alignment of their actions and behaviours with the company's core values. Include specific examples of how employees have demonstrated these values in their daily work, projects, or interactions.

Top Tip 2: Goal Integration Integrate company values into individual performance goals and objectives. Assess how well employees have incorporated these values into achieving their targets and contributing to the overall success of the organisation. Reward performance using the correct motivational rewards.

Top Tip 3: 360-Degree Feedback Gather feedback not only from direct supervisors but also from peers, subordinates, and other stakeholders.

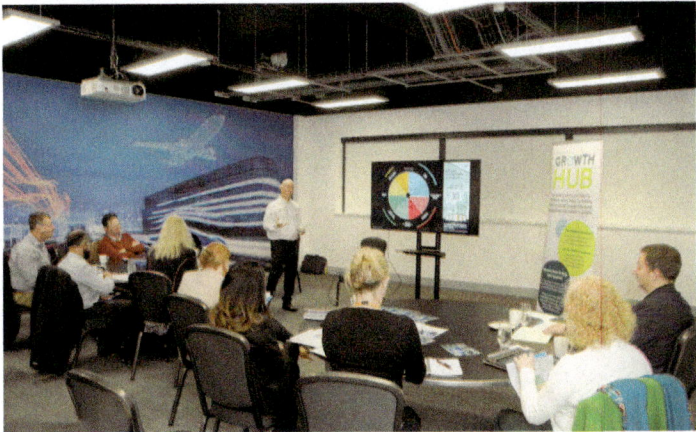

Leaders discussing the consequences and rewards of values.

CONCLUSION AND NEXT STEPS

In concluding this journey towards becoming an employer of choice, it's essential to recognise that attracting and retaining top talent is the key to consistency and growth in any business. Simply put: it's the people that make a business what it is.

When a Fortune-500 CEO was asked why his company was so successful, he replied "They come up in the lift everyday."

Through the process outlined in this book, you've assessed your current standing on the employee engagement wheel, gaining insights into your perceived strengths and weaknesses.

Remember, this assessment is a tool for self-reflection and discussion rather than a means of criticism.

Engaging with your leadership team, or indeed across the entire organisation, provides an opportunity for rich debate, leading to actionable insights.

Now, let's view your organisation through the lens of attracting and retaining talent.

Talented individuals seek a workplace with a compelling story, a clear vision, engaged leadership, motivational challenges, a culture of open communication, and a set of values that align with their own.

Understanding these aspects allows you to identify areas for improvement and the opportunity to implement positive changes.

You can now discuss these findings with your colleagues and refer to the relevant questions in this book to understand why these aspects are crucial for success.

Whether you choose to address these issues independently or seek assistance, the next steps are crucial for your organisation's transformation.

For those seeking my assistance, I've developed a streamlined methodology based on my experience working with numerous organisations, some recognised as award winning world leaders at employee engagement.

The Employee Engagement Programme, inspired by successful sessions conducted globally, initially comprises of two days of deep discovery and setup, followed by planning and execution.

These two days are highly recommended and set the foundation for your journey toward becoming an employer of choice.

However, serious organisations often invest further.

A 90-day motivational action planning programme ensures employees maintain and boost motivation, preventing talent loss and quiet quitting, whilst boosting productivity and morale.

Additionally, leadership and management training spread over four days over several months, ensures that your leaders and leadership team possess the necessary skills to drive consistency and quality across the business.

In total, I typically spend eight days, sometimes more, with each organisation committed to becoming an employer of choice.

If you are serious about transforming your workplace, I invite you to consider this comprehensive approach.

By working together, you are only eight days away from becoming that employer of choice and achieving your goal.

I'd love to embark on this journey together and make your vision of becoming an employer of choice a reality.

Thank you for buying my book and I sincerely hope it helps you in your quest to become an employer of choice. Maybe we will have the opportunity to work together and increase your organisation's success. Who knows?

Companies that invest in their people will fly!

For more information, contact Skills for Business Training Ltd:

www.skillsforbusinesstraining.co.uk

Email: steve@skillsforbusinesstraining.co.uk

Tel: 07971 882628

For more information about the 8 days of training, scan the QR code:

ACKNOWLEDGEMENTS

A heartfelt acknowledgment is due to Kim, my partner, whose unwavering support has been the cornerstone of my journey. Her encouragement and understanding have granted me the freedom to engage with clients and dedicate time to writing books, including this one. This book is as much a product of her support as it is of my own efforts.

Special gratitude goes to David Martinson for the book cover, and for his instrumental role in bringing the 'Employer of Choice' Wheel to life, a tool that underpins the whole book. Also Daniel Priestley, without whom the Wheel would not exist.

A tip of the hat to Joseph Sale too for his steadfast dedication to the editing process, ensuring the smooth transition of this book onto the shelves of Amazon. His commitment to excellence has been pivotal in refining the final product.

To Paul Bennett for kindly agreeing to Foreword this book and for his support over the years.

Last but certainly not least, my gratitude extends to all the clients who have placed their trust in me over the years, allowing me the privilege to work within the fabric of their businesses. Your trust has been the catalyst for the experiences shared within these pages.

With deep appreciation.

ABOUT THE AUTHOR

Steve, the author of "How to Become an Employer of Choice," has always been passionate about performance and helping individuals achieve their best. His early years were marked by his role as a performance coach in various sporting disciplines, a testament to his commitment to optimising human potential.

Notably, Steve played a pivotal role in the management team of Fitness First Plc during its remarkable transformation from a handful of clubs on the south coast of England to the world's largest independent health club chain. In just seven years, the company soared through the AIM and into the top 250 FTSE, showcasing both the challenges and triumphs of rapid growth.

Reflecting on this period, Steve acknowledges the complexities of fast growth but emphasises the invaluable lessons learned in building robust teams quickly. After leaving Fitness First Plc, he transitioned into coaching businesses on growth strategies, drawing on his extensive experience.

Steve's journey took an interesting turn when he joined Shirlaws, a fast growth business coaching firm from Australia, setting up operations in the UK. His exposure to the frameworks, tools, and techniques of Shirlaws, combined with his first-hand experience of rapid growth, equipped him with a unique toolkit.

In 2001, Steve founded Skills for Business Training Ltd, focusing on motivation, leadership, and employee engagement challenges that hindered true business growth. Simultaneously, as the UK government recognised the poor state of employee engagement, Steve found himself at the forefront of change.

Invited by the government to co-chair a task force addressing employee engagement, Steve played a vital role in studying successful companies and identifying four key themes crucial for success. These themes formed the basis for a course designed to help businesses unleash the full potential and capabilities of their people.

Steve's commitment to fostering engagement bore fruit as he collaborated with fast-growth businesses, transforming their people management and success. This journey led Steve to co-author an academic book titled "Mapping Motivation for Engagement" with James Sale, launching under Routledge's Publishing banner in vibrant Covent Garden, London.

Having spoken and conducted workshops globally, Steve continuously refines and enhances his offerings to address the modern challenges faced by leaders and managers. His latest masterpiece, "How to Become an Employer of Choice," is not just a culmination of Steve's expertise; it's a guiding light for leaders navigating the intricate landscape of attracting and retaining talent, to sustain growth, in the ever-evolving business terrain.

X x.com/skills4business
in linkedin.com/in/stevejonesmotivation

Printed in Great Britain
by Amazon